COLLECTANEA CHEMICA:

Being

Certain Select Treatises

on

Alchemy and Hermetic Medicine

By

Eirenaeus Philalethes, Dr. Francis Anthony, George Starkey, Sir George Ripley, and a Work by an Anonymous Unknown Which is Attributed to Edward Kelly

Table of Contents

THE SECRET OF THE IMMORTAL LIQUOR ALKAHEST

AURUM POTABILE

THE TRUE OIL OF SULPHUR

THE STONE OF THE PHILOSOPHERS

THE BOSOM BOOK OF SIR GEORGE RIPLEY

THE PREPARATION OF THE SOPHIC MERCURY

Prefatory Note.

The Hermetic Tracts comprised in this volume are printed from a quarto manuscript (itself a transcript from an older but now untraceable work) belonging to the celebrated collection of the late Mr. Frederick Hockley, who was well known among modern students of the secret sciences, not only for the resources of his Hermetic library, but for his practical acquaintance with many branches of esoteric lore, and for his real or reputed connection with the numerous but unavowed associations which now, as at anterior periods, are supposed to dispense initiation into occult knowledge. While practically the reprint is verbatim, it would have been a needless source of confusion, in a subject which is already sufficiently confused, to have reproduced the obsolete orthography, the superfluous capitals, the perplexing parentheses, the unnecessary italics, and the chaotic punctuation of the original. These, therefore, have been abandoned in favour of a simpler method. But the flavour of antiquity is sometimes valued for its age rather than its excellence; and partly in deference to this prejudice, there has been no attempt to reconstruct the style of these old writings. Moreover, though somewhat barbarous and entangled, it does not present sufficient difficulties to justify a drastic purgation.

THE SECRET
OF THE
IMMORTAL LIQUOR
CALLED
ALKAHEST
OR
IGNIS-AQUA.

By EIRENÆUS PHILALETHES.

Communicated to his Friend, a Son of Art, and now Philosopher. By Question and Answer.

THE SECRET OF THE LIQUOR ALKAHEST.

1. Question.—What is the Alkahest?
Answer.—It is a Catholic and Universal *Menstruum*, and, in a word, may be called (*Ignis-Aqua*) a Fiery Water, an uncompounded and immortal *ens*, which is penetrative, resolving all things into their first Liquid Matter, nor can anything resist its power, for it acteth without any reaction from the patient, nor doth it suffer from anything but its equal, by which it is brought into subjection; but after it hath dissolved all other things, it remaineth entire in its

former nature, and is of the same virtue after a thousand operations as at the first.

2. Q.—Of what substance is it?

A.—It is a noble circulated salt, prepared with wonderful art till it answers the desires of an ingenious artist; yet it is not any corporal salt made liquid by a bare solution, but is a saline spirit which heat cannot coagulate by evaporation of the moisture, but is of a spiritual uniform substance, volatile with a gentle heat, leaving nothing behind it; yet is not this spirit either acid or alkali, but salt.

3. Q.—Which is its equal?

A.—If you know the one, you may without difficulty know the other; seek therefore, for the Gods have made Arts the reward of industry.

4. Q.—What is the next matter of the Alkahest?

A.—I have told you that it is a salt; the fire surrounded the salt and the water swallowed up the fire, yet overcame it not; so is made the philosopher's fire, of which they speak; the vulgar burn with fire, we with water.

5. Q.—Which is the most noble salt?

A.—If you desire to learn this, descend into yourself, for you carry it about with you, as well the salt as its Vulcan, if you are able to discern it.

6. Q.—Which is it, tell me, I pray you?

A.—Man's blood out of the body, or man's urine, for the urine is an excrement separated, for the greatest part, from the blood. Each of these give both a volatile and fixed salt; if you know how to collect and prepare it, you will have a most precious Balsam of Life.

7. Q.—Is the property of human urine more noble than the urine of any beast?

A.—By many degrees, for though it be an excrement only, yet its salt hath not its like in the whole universal nature.

8. Q.—Which be its parts?

A.—A volatile and more fixed; yet according to the variety of ordering it, these may be variously altered.

9. Q.—Are there any things in urine which are different from its inmost specific urinaceous nature?

A.—There are, viz., a watery phlegm, and sea salt which we take in with our meat; it remains entire and undigested in the urine, and by separation may be divided from it, which (if there be no sufficient use of it in the meat after a convenient time) ceaseth.

10. Q.—Whence is that phlegm, or insipid watery humidity?

A.—It is chiefly from our several drinks, and yet everything hath its own phlegm.

11. Q.—Explain yourself more clearly.

A.—You must know that the urine, partly by the separative virtue, is conveyed with what we drink to the bladder, and partly consists of a watery Teffas (an excrementitious humour of the blood), whence being separated by the odour of the urinaceous ferment, it penetrates most deeply, the saltness being unchanged, unless that the saltness of the blood and urine be both the same; so that whatsoever is contained in the urine besides salt is unprofitable phlegm.

12. Q.—How doth it appear that there is a plentiful phlegm in urine?

A.—Thus suppose; first, from the taste; secondly, from the weight; thirdly, from the virtue of it.

13. Q.—Be your own interpreter.

A.—The salt of urine contains all that is properly essential to the urine, the smell whereof is very sharp; the taste differs according as it is differently ordered, so that sometimes it is also salt with an urinaceous saltness.

14. Q.—What have you observed concerning the weight thereof?

A.—I have observed thus much, that three ounces, or a little more, of urine, taken from a healthy man, will moderately outweigh about eighty grains of fountain water, from which also I have seen a liquor distilled which was of equal weight to the said water, whence it is evident that most of the salt was left behind.

15. Q.—What have you observed of its virtue?

A.—The congelation of urine by cold is an argument that phlegm is in it; for the salt of urine is not so congealed if a little moistened with a liquid, though it be water.

16. Q.—But this same phlegm though most accurately separated by distillation, retains the nature of urine, as may be perceived both by the smell and taste.

A.—I confess it, though little can be discerned by taste, nor can you perceive more, either by smell or taste, than you may from salt of urine dissolved in pure water.

17. Q.—What doth pyrotechny teach you concerning urine?

A.—It teacheth this, to make the salt of urine volatile.

18. Q.—What is then left?

A.—An earthly, blackish, stinking dreg.

19. Q.—Is the spirit wholly uniform?

A.—So it appeareth to the sight, smell, and taste; and yet it containeth qualities directly contrary to each other.

20. Q.—Which be they?

A.—By one, through its innate virtue, the Dulech is coagulated; by the other, it is dissolved.

21. Q.—What further?

A.—In the coagulation of urine, its spirit of wine is discovered.

22. Q.—Is there such a spirit in urine?

A.—There is indeed, truly residing in every urine, even of the most healthful man, most of which may be prepared by Art.

23. Q.—Of what efficacy is this spirit?

A.—Of such as is to be lamented, and indeed may move our pity to mankind.

24. Q.—Why so?

A.—From hence the Dulech, its most fierce enemy, hath its original.

25. Q.—Will you give an example of this thing?

A.—I will. Take urine, and dissolve in it a convenient quantity of saltpetre. Let it stand a month; afterwards distil it, and there will come over a spirit which burns upon the tongue like a coal of fire. Pour this spirit on again, and cohobate it four or five times, abstracting every time not above half; so the spirit becometh most piercing, yet not in the least sharp; the heat which goeth out in the first distillation of the liquor, afterwards grows sensibly mild, and at length almost (if not altogether) vanisheth, and the second spirit may be perceived mild, both by the smell and taste, which in the former was most sharp.

26. Q.—What have you observed concerning the former spirit?

A.—If it be a little shaked, oily streaks appear sliding here and there, just as spirit of wine distils down the head of the alembic in streaks like veins.

27. Q.—What kind of putrefaction should the urine undergo that such a spirit may be got from it?

A.—In a heat scarce to be perceived by sense, in a vessel lightly closed, or covered rather; it may also be sometimes hotter, sometimes cooler, so that neither the heat nor cold exceed a due mean.

28. Q.—How may this winy spirit become most perspicuous?

A.–By such a putrefaction as causeth a ferment, and exciteth ebullition, which will not happen in a long time if the urine be kept in a wooden vessel, and in a place which is not hot, but yet keeps out the cold, as, suppose, behind a furnace in winter, where let it be kept till of itself a ferment arise in the urine and stirs up bubbles, for then you may draw from it a burning water which is somewhat winy.

29. Q.–Is there any other spirit of urine?

A.–There is; for urine, putrefied with a gentle heat, during the space of a fortnight or thereabouts, sends forth a coagulating spirit, which will coagulate well rectified *Aqua Vitæ*.

30. Q.–How is that spirit to be prepared which forms the Dulech of itself with a clear watery stalagma; and also that which dissolves the same?

A.–Urine putrefied for a month and a-half in a heat most like the heat of horse-dung will give you, in a fit vessel, each stillatitious stalagma according to your desire.

31. Q.–Doth every spirit coagulate the spirit of wine?

A.–By no means; this second spirit is observed to want that virtue.

32. Q.–What doth urine, thus ordered, contain besides the aforesaid spirits?

A.–Its more fixed urinaceous salt, and, by accident, foreign marine salt.

33. Q.–Can this more fixed salt be brought over the alembic, with a gentle heat, in form of a liquor?

A.–It may, but art and ingenuity are required.

34. Q.–Where is the phlegm?

A.–In the salt; for in the preparation of putrefaction, the salt, being putrefied in the phlegm, ascends together with it.

35. Q.–Can it be separated?

A.–It may, but not by every artist.

36. Q.—What will this spirit do when it is brought to this?

A.—Try, and you will wonder at what you shall see in the solution of bodies.

37. Q.—Is not this the Alkahest?

A.—This liquor cannot consist without partaking of the virtues of man's blood; and in urine the footsteps thereof are observable.

38. Q.—In urine, therefore, and blood the Alkahest lies hid?

A.—Nature gives us both blood and urine; and from the nature of these pyrotechny gives us a salt which art circulates into the circulated salt of Paracelsus.

Q.—You speak short.

39. A.—I will add this; the salt of blood ought so to be transmuted by the urinaceous ferment that it may lose its last life, preserve its middle life, and retain its saltness.

40. Q.—To what purpose is this?

A.—To manifest the excellency which is in man's blood above all other blood whatever, which is to be communicated to the urine (after an excrementitious liquor is separated from it), whence this urine excels all others in a wonderful virtue.

41. Q.—Why do you add urine?

A.—You must know that to transmute things a corruptive ferment is required, in which respect all other salts give place to the strong urinous salt.

42. Q.—Cannot the phlegm be collected apart from the salt?

A.—It may, if the urine be not first putrefied.

43. Q.—How great a part of the water is to be reckoned phlegm?

A.—Nine parts of ten, or thereabouts, distilled from fresh urine are to be rejected, the tenth part (as much as can be extracted in form of liquor) is to be kept; from that dried urine which remains in the bottom by a gentle fire (which will not cause sublimation), let the salt be extracted with water, so that there be as much water as half that urine whence this feces was dried; whatsoever is imbibed by the water, let it be poured off by decanting; let it be strained, or purged, per deliquium; then filter it through a glass. Let fresh water be poured on, and reiterate this work till the salt become pure, then join this vastly stinking salt with your last spirit and cohobate it.

PRAISED BE THE NAME OF THE LORD.—AMEN.

AURUM POTABILE:
OR THE
RECEIPT
OF
Dr. Fr. ANTONIE:
SHOWING
His Way and Method. How he made and prepared that most Excellent Medicine for the Body of Man.

DR. FR. ANTONIE'S RECEIPT,

Showing the way to make his most excellent medicine called "Aurum Potabile."

Take block tin, and burn it in an iron pan (making the pan red hot before you put it in), keeping a continual fire under it, and stirring it always till it be like unto ashes. Some will look red; it will be burning a day, or half-a-day at the least; it must be stirred with an iron coal rake, a little one, the handle two feet long.

G. H. M. made an iron pan a foot and a-half long and a foot broad, the brims two inches deep, and made an oven in a chimney with bars of iron in the bottom, whereon he placed the pan, and a place under to make fire; and it will after this manner sooner be burned (viz., half-a-day). The smoke will not hurt it.

These ashes keep in a glass close covered.

Take of these ashes four ounces and of the strongest red wine vinegar three pints, and put them in a glass like an urinal, the ashes being put in first; lute the vessel, and let it stand in a hot Balneum ten days, which ended, take it forth, and set it to cool, and let it stand two or three whole days that the feces may sink unto the bottom. The glass must be shaken six or seven times every day.

That which is clear let it run forth unfiltered by two or three woollen threads into a glass basin, and distil it in a glassen still till the liquor be stilled all forth. This distilled water put upon four ounces of fresh ashes, upon the ashes from which the first liquor was filtered; put also a quart of strong red wine vinegar; lute the glass as before, and put him into the Balneum, and there let him stand to digest ten days: filter this, and distil it as aforesaid. Thirdly, pour on those ashes one pint of the like vinegar, and put it in Balneum ten days: filter it, and distil it, as aforesaid. After the third infusion throw away the ashes.

Distil all the infusions apart, till the liquor be clean distilled forth.

Take this distilled water, as often as it is distilled, and pour it upon new ashes, keeping the weight and order; their infusions, filterings, and distillations reiterate seven times.

And you shall have of this water the menstruum sought for.

You must take heed that the vinegar be of red wine, and very strong, otherwise your menstruum will not perform your expectation.

The Bishop gave Dr. Antonie 30s. for a quart of menstruum.

Take an ounce of pure refined gold (which costs £3 13s. 4d.); cast it into a wedge and file it into small dust with a fine file. Put this ounce of filed gold into a calcined pot, and put to it so much white salt as will near fill the pot, and set it among charcoals where it may stand continually hot four hours (if it stand too hot the salt will melt). Which four hours ended, take it forth, and let it stand to cool; then put it on a painter's stone, and grind it very small with a muller. Then put it into the pot and calcine it, and grind it again till you have done it four or five times: if it look red and blue when you take it forth, it is perfect good.

After this calcining and grinding, put it into a glass basin, and put to it the basinful of scalding hot water, and stir it a good while, till the thick part is fully settled to the bottom. Then pour away that water, and put the like; stir it, and let it settle as before; and so do again, till the water, when it is settled, have no taste of salt. This will be doing two or three days.

Of this ounce of gold there will be hardly above sixteen or seventeen grains brought into fine white calx, but to separate it from the gold leave a little of the last fresh water in the basin, and stir it well together. The calx will swim to the top, which softly pour from the gold into another basin. If all the white calx go not forth, put a little more water and stir it again, and pour it into the basin to the other calx; then let it settle, and pour away almost all the water, and evaporate away all the rest over a heat till it be throughly dry. And so put it up into a. glass.

Then put the gold which is not yet calx to salt as aforesaid, and calcine it, and grind it four times again; and then wash it; and then take the calx from it as before; and the gold that remains calcine and wash as before, till it be all calx.

Take an ounce of this calx, and put it into an urinal-like glass, containing about a pint, and put to it half-a-pint of the menstruum. Set this glass in a hot Balneum six days (being close luted), and shake it often every day. When the six days are ended, let it stand two or three days; then pour away that which is clear very gently, for fear of troubling the feces. To these feces put fresh menstruum, but not fully so much as at the first; and so the third time, but not fully so much as at the second. Then take the dry feces, which are the calx, and keep them lest some tincture remain therein.

These coloured liquors put into a glass still, and distil them in a Balneum, at the first with a very gentle fire, till all that which is clear be run forth, and that which remain be as thick as honey. Then take it forth and set it to cool. Then put the glass into an earthen pot, and put ashes about the glass into the pot, and fix the pot into a little furnace fast, and make a fire under, so that the glass may stand very warm till the feces be black and very dry. You may look with a candle through the glass still, and see when it is risen with bunches and dry. Then take away your fire, and let the glass be very cold; then take out the black earth. This black earth being taken forth, put it into a glass basin, and grind it with the bottom of another round glass to powder. Then put it into an urinal-like glass, containing about a pint, and to that put a little above half-a-pint of the spirit of wine. Set this glass in a cold place till it be red, which will be about ten days. Shake it often every day, till within three days you pour it forth. Then pour away the clear liquor gently, and that clear put into a glass still or other glass, till you have more. Then put more spirit of wine to those feces, and order it as before; and if that be much coloured, put *Spiritus Vini*, to it the third time, as at the first. Put all these coloured liquors together and distil them till the feces (called the tincture) be as thick as a syrup.

Take an ounce of this tincture, and put it into a pint of Canary sack, and so when it is clear you may drink of it, which will be about a day and a-half.

The Preparation of the Vinegar to make the Menstruum.

Glasses necessary: Get three or four glassen stills which will hold a gallon or two apiece, and a Balneum two feet and a-half square to hold many glasses. Get about six gallons of the strongest red wine vinegar (vinegar of claret or white wine is too weak), made of red wine, sack, or Muscadine, and set as many stills going at a time as your Balneum will hold. Take a pint of that which runneth first, and put it away, as weak and not fit for this use. Then still out all the rest, till the still be dry. Wash the still with a little of the (phlegm) the first running, and then wipe it dry. Then put in that which was distilled, and do as before, putting away the first pint; and so do five times. So of a gallon you shall have three pints of the spirit of vinegar, and of your six gallons only two gallons and two pints. And if your spirit be yet too weak distil it oftener.

This keep in a glass close stopped to make your menstruum with; you may stop it with cork, and leather over it.

You must provide three strong green glasses to make menstruum, with little mats round the bottoms, containing four pints apiece.

To lute them, fit a wooden stoppel of dry wood, first boiled, and then dried in an oven, to the mouth; then melt hard wax to fill the chinks; then paste a brown paper next over that; then prepare luting of clay, horsedung, and ashes, and stop over all that.

Glass Stills: Two or three to distil the first infusions on the earth; cover three or four pints apiece of green glass.

The rule of all stillings: You must paste brown paper to the closing of the head of the still, and also paste the receiver and nose of the still together so that no strength go forth.

Calcining Pots: Provide about a dozen, for many when they are put into a strong fire will break; then must you let your fire slack.

THE ADMIRABLE EFFICACY AND ALMOST INCREDIBLE VIRTUE
OF TRUE
OIL WHICH IS MADE OF SULPHUR VIVE SET ON FIRE
AND COMMONLY CALLED
OIL OF SULPHUR
PER CAMPANAM.
BY
GEORGE STARKEY.

THE OIL OF SULPHUR.

Of this most noble liquor, and not vulgar medicine, the noble Helmont writeth thus, in his excellent discourse concerning THE TREE OF LIFE. In the year 1600 a certain man belonging to the camp, whose office was to keep account of the provision of victuals which was made for the army, being charged with a numerous family of small children unable to shift for themselves, himself being then fifty-eight years of age, was very sensible of the great care and burden which lay upon him to provide for them while he lived, and concluded that, should he die, they must be enforced to beg their bread from door to door: whereupon he came (saith Helmont) and desired of me something for the preservation of his life. I then (being a young man) pitied his sad condition, and thus thought with myself: The fume of burning sulphur is, by experience, found powerfully effectual to preserve wines from corruption. Then I, recollecting my thoughts, concluded that the acid liquor of oil, which is made of sulphur vive, set on fire, doth of necessity contain in itself this fume; yea, and the whole odour of the sulphur, inasmuch as it is indeed nothing else but the very sulphureous fume imbibed, or drunk up in its mercurial salt, and so becomes a condensed liquor. Then I thought with myself: Our blood being (to us) no other than, as it were, the very wine of our life, that being preserved, if it prolong not the life, at least it will keep it sound from those many diseases which proceed originally from corruption: by which means the life being sound, and free from diseases, and defended from pains and griefs, might be in some sort spun out into a further length than otherwise. Upon which meditated resolution I gave him a vial glass, with a small quantity of this oil, distilled from sulphur vive burning, and taught him (moreover) how to make it as he should afterwards need it. I advised him of this liquor he should take two drops before each meal in a small draught of beer, and not, ordinarily, to exceed that dose, nor to intermit the use of it, taking for granted that two drops of that oil, contained a large quantity of the fume of sulphur. The man took my advice, and at this day, in the year 1641, he is lusty and in good health, walks the streets at Brussels without complaint, and is likely longer to live; and that which is most remarkable, in this whole space of forty-one years he was not so much as ill, so as to keep his bed; yea, although (when of great age) in the depth of winter, he broke his leg, near to his ankle bone, by a fall upon the ice, yet with the use of the oil he recovered, without the least symptom of a fever; and although in his old age poverty had reduced him to great straits and hardship, and made him feel much want of things necessary for the comfort and conveniency of life, yet he lives, healthy and sound, though spare and lean. The old man's name is John Moss, who waited upon Rithovius, Bishop of Ypres, in his chamber, where the Earls of Horne and Egmondon were beheaded by the Duke of Alva; and he was then twenty-five years of age, so that now he is complete ninety-nine years of age, healthy and lusty, and still continues the use of that liquor daily. Thus far Helmont, which relation, as it is most remarkable, so it gives the philosophical reason of his advice, on which it was grounded. And elsewhere the same author relates how by this liquor he cured many dangerous, deplorable fevers, which by other doctors had been given over for desperate. And in other places he commends it as a peerless remedy to assuage the intolerable thirst which accompanies most fevers.

To which relation and testimony of this most learned doctor and acute philosopher I shall add my own experience.

I find it a rare preservative against corruption, not only in living creatures, but even in dead flesh, beer, wine, ale, etc.; a recoverer of dying beer and wines that are decayed, a cure for beer when sick and roping. Flesh by this means may be preserved so incorruptible as no embalming in the world can go beyond it for the keeping of a dead carcase, nor salting come near its efficacy; as to the conserving meat, or fowls, or fish, which by this means are not only kept from corruption, but made a mumial balsam, which is itself a preservative against corruption of such as shall eat thereof; which being a curious rarity, and too costly to be made a vulgar experiment, I shall pass it over, and come to those cases which are most beneficial and desirable.

It is an excellent cleanser of the teeth: being scoured with it, they will become as white as the purest ivory, and the mouth being washed with oil dropped in water or white wine, so as to make it only of the sharpness of vinegar, it prevents the growing of that yellow scale which usually adheres to the teeth, and is the forerunner of their putrefaction; it prevents their rottenness for the future, and stops it (being begun) from going further, takes away the pain of the teeth, diverts rheums, and is a pure help for the savour of the breath, making it very sweet. In a word, there is not a more desirable thing can be found for such who would have clear or sound teeth, or sweet breath, or to be free from rheums: for which use let the water be made by dropping this oil into it, as sharp as vinegar, as I said before.

Against a tickling cough, or hoarseness, it is a rare remedy, not only taken two or three drops twice a day inwardly, in the usual drink one useth before each meal, but also by gargling the throat with it; and (so used) it is excellent against swelled throats, anginas, strumas, palates of the mouth inflamed, or the uvula of the throat, or the almonds of the ears, which are (usually said then to be) fallen. It is excellent also against the headache, and to divert rheums from the eyes, to wash the temples therewith; likewise to take away tetters, morphew, or scabs, this dropped into water is a pleasant, safe, and effectual remedy.

Besides which outward applications, it is a Lord internally taken, preventing corruption, rooting out the seeds thereof, though never so deeply concealed in the body, and, upon that score, opening inveterate obstructions, eradicating old pains, and preventing otherwise usual relapses into stranguretical, colical, or arthritical pains: it is abstersive, cleansing all excrementitious, settlings in the mesaraic or mesenterial vessels, and so cutting off the original source, and taking away the cause of putrefactive corruption, which is the productive beginner of very many diseases.

On this score it lengthens the life, and frees the body from many pains and ails to which it otherwise would be subject.

It is a pleasant remedy, having only a little sharpness, which to the palate is most grateful; and yet this acidity is contradistinct from that acidity which is the forerunner of putrefaction, which it kills and destroys, as the acidity of the spirit of vitriol is destroyed by the fixed acrimony of its own *caput mortuum*, or that of vinegar by the touch of ceruse or minium.

Preternatural heat and thirst in fevers are in no way allayed so speedily, and easily, as by this, nor is there anything which for a constant continuance may be more safely and profitably taken. Spirit of salt (such as the noble Helmont speaks of) alone may be joined with this, for its safety and continual use with profit, especially in nephritical distempers, and the heat or sharpness of urine.

Now, as this is so noble a medicine, so there is none in the world more basely adulterated and counterfeited, our wise doctors commending for it (*quid pro quo*) an adulterated mineral acidity of vitriol, distilled in a retort from vulgar sulphur, which the apostate chemists prepare and sell for, and the knavish apothecaries use and give to their patients, instead of this true spirit, which if sincere is clear as water, ponderous, and exquisitely acid, made of sulphur vive only, set on fire without any other mixture, and the fumes received in a broad glass, fitted for the purpose, vulgarly called a campana or bell, from its shape or likeness.

Most sottish is that maxim of the doctors, that spirit of sulphur and vitriol are of one nature, when experience teacheth that mere acetosity of vitriol (which brings over nothing of its excellent virtue) will dissolve argent vive, which the strongest spirit of sulphur, truly and not sophistically made, will not touch, nor will that recover beer or wines, or preserve them, as this will do: one, therefore, is an unripe esurine acetosity, of little virtue; the other a balsam of antidotary virtue, a preservative against corruption, and, upon that score, nothing can be used more effectually as a preservative against, or a remedy in, contagious fevers, small-pox, measles, or pestilence than this, nor more ridiculously than the other, which being drawn from the vulgar sulphur, that hath an infection of malignity mixed with it (which it took from the arsenical nature of the minerals from which it was melted), adds nothing to the virtue of the crude vitriolate spirits, but only that which was before of little virtue, to become a medicine of more danger and hazard, but not a jot more goodness than it was, when first wandr from the vitriol; which being of itself clear and crude, is for to deceive the ignorant (by its colour) tinctured with some root or bark. Thus the credulous world is imposed upon and cheated, while, instead of most noble remedies (in name promised), adulterated trifles are produced, to the disparagement of art, and the scandal and reproach of the professor's medicine. To discover which abuses and vindicate the art, I have made my preludium, concerning this oil or spirit of sulphur, the virtues of which (if truly and faithfully made) are so eminently remarkable, and almost incredibly efficacious, that I thought it not unworthy my pains in a few lines to communicate to the studious reader both what real benefit is to be expected from the true and what injury is clone to the deluded (at least), if not destroyed, patients by the sophisticate oil of sulphur.

Postscript.

That those who desire this so pleasant, so efficacious, and profitable a remedy may not be abused by the base counterfeit oil of vitriol, corruptly called oil of sulphur, because it has been once distilled from common unwholesome brimstone, and tincted with some bark or root of which the town is full, and all apothecaries' shops, to the great abuse of art, but much greater of those who make use of it instead of the true, when indeed it hath not one quality like thereto; let the reader be informed that at George Starkey's house, in St. Thomas Apostle's, next door to Black Lion Court; and at Richard Johnson's, at the Globe in Montague Close, in Southwark, the true is to be had, drawn from sulphur vive (set on fire), without any addition but the sulphur itself, which is easily known by its clearness, sharpness, weight, not working on quicksilver, turning bitter like to gall on the filings of silver, preserving wine and beer from corruption, restoring then when decayed, and, in a word, by its quenching feverish heat and thirst, etc. As before hath been rehearsed at large, it may by anyone be distinguished from that which is false and sophisticate. However, at those two places he may be confident of that which is real and true. And likewise at Richard Johnson's house in Montague Close, in Southwark, aforesaid, you may have any chemical salts, oils, and spirits. Besides which oil or spirit of sulphur, several other rare and admirably effectual medicinal secrets for the certain, safe, and speedy cure of most, if not all diseases, as hath been proved by many hundred patients (adjudged rather incurable or desperately dangerous by other doctors), are there to be had, being more than ordinary secrets and preparations of George Starkey, who entitles himself a Philosopher by the Fire.

And in particular that pill, or antidote injuriously challenged as an invention of Richard Matthews, who, in truth, had that preparation (for which he hath since been so famous) from the said George Starkey, the true author thereof, who had it from God, by studious search, without help of book or master; and which preparation he hath since amended and advanced in virtue beyond comparison of that which Mr. Matthews had from him, as hath been, and is daily, confirmed by the experience of able men.

Concerning which antidote, or pill, or rather anodinous elixir, its virtues and advancement, to almost a true universality, by four variations thereof, which the first author of the thing (by long experience) found out, he hath wrote, particularly, and at large, with the way of administering it and how to order the patient, by one and all of these preparations, for his recovery out of any of the most desperately acute, or fixed chronical diseases; which book being now ready for the press, in a few days, God willing, shall see the light. It is called "A Brief Examination and Censure of Several Medicines, etc."

For the undeceiving of such as have been injuriously and falsely persuaded that only Mr. Richard Matthews and Paul Hobson have that medicine truly prepared, condemning all others as counterfeit, to the disparagement and palpable injury of the first inventor, who counts it unreasonable that he who learned what he had from him should censure himself as a counterfeit, unless he bind himself up to his preparation, which, though it be a true one, yet is the most inferior in virtue of all the author knows, and called by him his "Elixir Diaphoretick Commune." Of which able, judicious practitioners (having once bought his more effectual and higher graduated preparations in the same kind) have so low an esteem (comparatively to these others) that they desire no more thereof. Farewell.

GEORGE STARKEY.

When this treatise and the postscript were written, Mr. Starkey then lived in the place therein specified; but he died, as I have been informed, of the sickness, Anno. Dom. 1665, by venturing to anatomise a corpse dead of the plague, as Mr. Thomson, the chemist, had done before him, and lived many years after; but Mr. Starkey's adventure cost him his life. However, the medicine, truly made and prepared from the mineral sulphur, called sulphur vive, may now be had of very many chemists in and about London; nay, the difficulty in making thereof is not so great but that you may make it yourself if you please, and if you do but wait the time and opportunity to buy the mineral sulphur (not common brimstone), for the mineral is not to be had at all times.

The process and shape for the glass bell, and the manner of making and rectifying this spirit from the mineral sulphur, or sulphur vive, as it comes stone-like out of the earth, may be seen in the chemical works of Hartman and Crollius, called "ROYAL CHYMISTRY," Chara's "Royal Pharmacopæa," Lefehure, Thibault, Lemery, Glaser, Shroder's "Dispensatory," and many others, unto whom I refer you.—W. C. B.

THE STONE OF THE PHILOSOPHERS:
EMBRACING
THE FIRST MATTER
And the Dual Process for the Vegetable and Metallic Tinctures.

THE CONTENTS.

CHAPTER I. Introduction.
CHAPTER II. Of the Vegetable Tincture, or the Process called the Lesser Circulation.
CHAPTER III. Of the Uses of the Vegetable Tincture, with some general remarks on their great efficacy in Medicine.
CHAPTER IV. Of the Metallic Tincture.
CHAPTER V. Of the Second Matter, or Seed in Metals.
CHAPTER VI. Of the Dissolution and Extraction of the Seed in Metals.
CHAPTER VII. Of the Separation and Further Treatment of our Philosophical Seed.
CHAPTER VIII. Of the Union, or Mystical Marriage, in the Philosophical Process.
CHAPTER IX. Of the Further Treatment and Ripening of our Seed.
CHAPTER X. Of the Further Process towards the Ripening of our Noble Seed.
CHAPTER XI. A Further Description of the Process.
CHAPTER XII. Of the Stone and its Uses.
CHAPTER XIII. Of the Transmutation.

THE PREFACE.

IF there had been any English publication upon this curious and momentous subject, easy to be met with, that deserved regard, the public had not been troubled with this. The operations herein described are all within the compass of Nature; they are laid down in plain language, and the reasoning upon them is suited to a common apprehension, where there is a chemical turn of mind. Anyone inclining to these studies, if poor, will do well to mind his proper business, without attempting the Philosophical Work, as the necessary apparatus must require more expense and time than he can spare; but such as are of ability may well undertake it, both as a recreation and useful employment, in which an ingenious labourer may be retained as an assistant for the manual operations, at such a daily allowance as may be proportioned to his labour and sufficient for a subsistence. No more can be expected by a man who is modest and pious: one that is vicious can never be depended upon in a work of consequence like this, where patience is a main requisite, together with a punctilious veracity in reciting every variation of the matter during a tedious process from seven to nine months.

Whoever will therefore undertake this process must needs have an assistant; and, we again repeat it, such an one whose fidelity, above all things, may be safely relied upon; true, faithful, and religious; being, like his employer, acute to investigate the phenomena of Nature, especially in chemical processes.

Those who are accustomed to treat this science with contempt may doubtless ridicule anything written expressly upon it without examining what is advanced in its support, the title only of a book being of a sufficient reason with many for their disregarding the contents. We shall leave such superficial people in quiet possession of that unhappy self-sufficiency they have acquired, and rather apologise for the plainness with which this process is delivered to those possessors of it, if any, and yet alive, who may be displeased with our public spirit in communicating what has so long been considered as a sacred deposition with a few Philosophers.

CHAPTER I.
The Introduction.

  BECAUSE many have written of the Philosopher's Stone without any knowledge of the art, and the few books extant, written by our learned predecessors and true masters hereupon, are either lost or concealed in the collections of such (however despised) as are lovers and seekers of natural secrets, we have taken a resolution to communicate our knowledge in this matter, to the intent that those who are convinced the Philosophical Work is no fiction, but grounded in the possibility of Nature, may be faithfully directed in their studies, and have an undoubted criterion to distinguish between such authors as are genuine sons of science and those who are spurious, as writing by hearsay only.

  We shall not on this occasion give a summary of their names who are undoubted masters in the art, but shall take occasion to introduce them, as it may be necessary, in the following chapters; and as their sense is often concealed under a studied ambiguity of expression, we shall, out of the gift which the Almighty hath dispensed to us, declare plainly, and without any reserve, the first matter of the

Philosopher's Stone, the manner of proceeding through the whole process, both in the Vegetable and Metallic Tinctures, beginning with the Vegetable process first, as the most easy and simple, yet well worthy the attention of all ingenious persons, particularly the practical chemists and preparers of medicines.

CHAPTER II.

Of the Vegetable Tincture, or the Process called the Lesser Circulation.

VERY few of the true philosophers have touched upon this subject, for it seemed trifling in respect to the great work, as the process in metals is generally termed; but there is a modern publication in English, a small thin duodecimo, without any author's name, having for its title "*Aphorisms, seu Circulus majus et Circulus minus,*" wherein the whole process is plainly laid down.

This book is written by an undoubted master in the art; and no treatise, ancient or modern, is so explicit in the directions for conducting the great work. The directions are very short, but much to the purpose, provided the reader has an idea what part of the work is alluded to. The author, agreeable to his title, delivers his doctrine by way of aphorisms. But to return from this digression.

We proposed in this chapter to lay open the vegetable process, as a clue to the more important work in the mineral kingdom. A certain person, who is now living, and advertises balsam of honey, tincture of sage, etc., has turned his studies this way; and from his great abilities as a professed physician and botanist, has convinced all unprejudiced persons that noble tinctures may be extracted from vegetables. We hope this gentleman will not despise our free communication, both to him and the public, if we show the insufficiency of his method, though it is ingenious, while we establish the rationale of ours on the never-failing ground of truth and philosophy.

He observes, with a precision which can only result from numerous trials, that different herbs impart their tinctures in such proportions of alcohol as he has found out. It is allowed that the volatile spirit and balsamic sulphur are thus extracted; but there are the essential, or fixed, salt and sulphur of the herb yet left in the process. These require another management to extract, which he is either ignorant of, or is so disingenuous as to conceal from the public; but that so noble a secret may lie open to all for a general advantage, here follows a plain account of the vegetable work.

Take any herb which is potent in medicine, and either extract the tincture with spirit of wine, or distil in the common way; reserve the distilled water, or tincture, when separated from the fæces, for use. Then take the feces, or *Caput Mortuum*, and calcine it to a calx. Grind this to powder. That done, take the water, or tincture, and mix them together; distil again, and calcine, forcing the moisture over by a retort, in a wary process, calcining and cohobating the spirit on the salt till it attains a perfect whiteness and oily nature, like the finest alkali, commonly called Flemish. As your salt requires it in the process, have in readiness more of the extracted tincture, or distilled spirit, that you may not work it, viz., the salt, too dry; and yet proceed cautiously, not adding too much of the moisture, so that the dealbation, or whitening, may keep visibly heightening at every repetition of the process. Frequent experiments may enable you to push it on to a redness, but a fine yellow is the best of all; for the process tends, in its perfection at this period, to a state of dryness, and must be managed with a strong fire. By following these directions, you have here the two tinctures in the Vegetable Kingdom, answering to the white and red tinctures in the mineral.

CHAPTER III.

Of the Uses of the Vegetable Tinctures, with some general remarks on their great efficacy in medicine.

You have, by carefully following our directions above, procured the tinctures, white or yellow, in the Vegetable Kingdom. The yellow is more efficacious if the work is well performed; either of them, by being exposed in the air, will soon run into a thick, essential oil, smelling very strong of the plant, and the virtues of any quantity may be concentered by often repeating the circulation. But you have no need of this, unless for curiosity, there being in your tinctures a real permanent power to extract the essential virtues of any herb you may require on immersion only, where the essential salt and volatile spirit, together with the sulphureous oil, are all conjoined, floating on they-top of your tincture, and the terrestrial feces precipitated to the bottom; not as in distillation, or extraction of the tincture with alcohol, while the stalk and texture of the plant are entire; no, this Vegetable Tincture devours the whole substance of the plant, and precipitates only the earthy particles acquired in its vegetation, which no degree of calcination could push to an alkali, without its essential salt.

Such is the virtue of our Vegetable Tincture; and if the operation be never so often repeated with different herbs, it loses nothing of its virtue, or quantity or quality, casting up the virtues of whatever herb is immersed, and precipitating the earth as before, when both are easily separated and the medicine preserved for use. Let a medicine, thus prepared, be examined, and the principles by which it is extracted, with the general methods of preparation; if the distilled water, for instance, of any aromatical or balsamic herb, be took, common experience will convince us that nothing but its volatile parts come over the head; but take the *Caput Mortuum*, and it will calcine after this process, and afford an alkali, which proves itself to be an essential salt by its pungency, and will, in the air, run to an oil, which is its essential sulphur. If you take the tincture extracted with alcohol, it is the same, only the more resinous parts of sonic herbs may enrich the extract, and the volatile sulphur giving the colour and scent, be retained, which escapes in distillation; but the potent virtue or soul of the herb, if we may be allowed the expression, goes to the dunghill. It is the same if the expressed juice of the herb is used; and if taken in powder, or substance, as it is sometimes prescribed, but little of its virtue, beyond its nourishing quality, can be communicated to the patient, except as a bitter or a vermifuge, in which cases, perhaps, it is best by way of infusion.

    Let none despise the operation above laid down, because it is not to be found in the ordinary books of chemistry; but consider the possibility of Nature, who brings about wonderful effects by the most simple causes: neither let any imagine this process so easy as to perform it without some trials, patiently attending to her operations and endeavouring to account for any deficiency in the course of his work. For this reason it will be proper that the artist forms to himself an idea what the intention is to procure, how far Nature has prepared his matter to work upon, in what state she has left it, and how far it may be exalted above the ordinary point of virtue, which it could attain in the crude air, and this by the Philosophic Art assisting Nature, as a handmaid, with an administration of due heat, which is nutritive and not corrosive A recapitulation of the foregoing process, with some remarks on the different stages, will be sufficient here to explain our meaning above, and prepare the reader for what follows concerning the metallic tincture, or Stone of the Philosophers.

The virtues of herbs and simples are confessedly great and manifold; among these, some are poisonous and narcotic, yet of great use in medicine; none of them but want some preparation or correction. Now the common ways of doing this are defective; neither preserving the virtue entire, nor furnishing any menstruum capable of doing it with expedition and certainty. Alcohol, as was before observed, will extract a tincture and distillation a spirit. We reject neither of these methods in our work, as they are useful to decompound the subject; but we are not content with a part of its virtues.

To speak philosophically, we would have its soul, which is its Essential Salt, and its spirit, which is the inflammable sulphur. The body in which these resided we are not concerned for; it is mere earth, and must return from whence it came: whereas the soul and spirit are paradisiacal, if the artist can free them from their earthy prison without loss; but this can only be done by death. Understand us aright. Philosophically speaking, no more is meant than decomposition of the subject into its first principles, as the uniting them more permanently with an increase of virtue is most emphatically called a resurrection and regeneration. Now this decompounding is to be done with judgment, so as not to corrode or destroy, but divide the matter into its integral parts. At this period of the work the artist will consider what is further intended, keeping Nature in view, who, if she is properly assisted in her operations, produces from the dissolution of any subject something more excellent, as in a grain of corn, or any vegetable seed, which by cultivation may be pushed to a surprising produce; but then it must die first, as our Blessed Saviour very emphatically observes: and let this saying dwell upon the artist's imagination, that he may know what he generally intends; for the whole philosophical work, both in vegetables and minerals, is only a mortifying of the subject, and reviving it again to a more excellent life.

Now if the intention in the foregoing process was to increase simply any vegetable in its kind, the destruction and revivification must follow the ordinary course of vegetation by the medium of seed; and Nature can only be assisted by fertilising the soil, together with a proper distribution of heat and moisture. Yet there are not wanting authors, and particularly Paracelsus, who boldly describe processes wherein the vital quality of the seed has been destroyed by calcination, and yet brought to life again at the pleasure of an artist. Such reveries are a scandal to philosophy, and a snare to the superficial reader, who is generally more struck with impossibilities, roundly asserted, than the modesty of true artists. These confess their operations are within the bounds of Nature, whose limits they cannot surpass.

The reader, then, will consider that our intention here is not to increase the seminal quality, but to concentre, in a little compass, the medicinal virtues of a herb. Nature is desirous of this in all her productions, but can only rise to such a point of perfection, in her ordinary course, through the crudity of the air and fixing power of the elements. Now if we take the vegetables at that point of perfection to which she has pushed them, and farther assist her in decompounding, purifying, uniting, and reviving the subject, we obtain, what she could not otherwise produce, a real permanent tincture, the quintessence, as it is called, or such a harmonious mixture of the four elementary qualities as constitutes a fifth, from thenceforth indissoluble, and not to be debased with any impurity.

But the virtue of this Vegetable Tincture is capable of improvement *ad infinitum*, in its own kind, by adding more of its spirit or extracted tincture, and repeating the circulation, which is every time more speedily finished, as there is a magnetical quality in the fixed salt, and essential oil, which assimilates to itself all the real virtues of what is added, only rejecting the feculent, earthy qualities; so that in a grain of the tincture much virtue may be concentered, not at all corrosive or ardent, but friendly to the animal life, and most powerful as a medicine for disorders which the herb is appropriated to cure. Nay, something of this nature was still sought for by the distillers of ardent spirits, when phlegm has been drawn away from the volatile sulphur, till it became proof spirit, as it is termed, which will burn dry, a plain indication that it contained nothing essential in it from the subject out of which it was extracted; for that which is essential cannot be destroyed by the fire, but is reddened to an alkaline salt, having in its centre an Incombustible Sulphur, which, on exposing to the air, manifests itself both to the sight and touch. Now, if this Salt and Sulphur are purified sufficiently, and the distilled spirit, or extracted tincture, added, Nature finds a subject wherein she can carry her operations to the highest limit, if an artist furnishes her with proper vessels, and a degree of heat suitable to her intentions.

CHAPTER IV.
Of the Metallic Tincture.

WHEN we undertook a description of the vegetable process, it was chiefly with a view to familiarise the reader to a general idea of the Philosophic Work in metals, as both proceed upon the same principles, only the mercuries of metals are more difficult to extract, and stronger degrees of heat are required, as well as more of the artist's time and patience; neither can he succeed in the operation without frequent trials, and a constant consideration within his mind as to what is within the possibility of Nature. For this purpose it is necessary to know the composition of metals, that he may know how to decompound and reduce them to their first principles, which is treated of very mysteriously by the philosophers, and purposely concealed, as the right key to unlock all the secrets of Nature. We shall be more explicit on this head, for the time draws near when, as Sendivogius has observed, the confection of the Stone will be discovered as plainly as the making of cheese from rennet. But we warn the reader not to imitate Midas in the fable, by seeking the noble tincture in metals out of covetousness; for the true wise men seek only a medicine for human infirmities, and esteem gold but as it furnishes them with the means of independence and the exercise of universal beneficence. They communicate their talents, without vain glory or ostentation, to such as are worthy searchers of Nature, but concealing their names as much as possible, while living, as well as their knowledge of the mystery from the world.

 We shall herein follow their example, and yet write more plainly of the Metallic Process than any of them has hitherto done, knowing that the providence of the Most High will effectually guard this Arcanum from falling into the hands of covetous gold seekers and knavish pretenders to the Art of Transmutation; because the first sort of men will, from their impatience, soon leave the simplicity of Nature for processes of more subtlety invented by the latter, and adapted to such avaricious views as the other have formed, who, judging of things by their own griping dispositions, know not the noble liberality of Nature, but imagine some gold must be advanced before she will replenish their heaps. This is well foreseen by those smoke sellers, who receive what they can catch, as if they were her proper agents; and, having no conscience to put a stop to their imposition, the deception is kept up till all vanishes in smoke.

 Let it be observed, then, that all who have written on the art, from undoubted principles, assert that the genuine process is not expensive; time and fuel, with manual labour, being all allowed for. Besides, the matter to be wrought upon is easy to procure by the consent of all. A small quantity of gold and silver is, indeed, necessary when the stone is made, as a medium for its tinging either in the white or red tinctures, which such pretenders have urged from books of philosophers as a plausible pretence to rob the avaricious both of their time and money; but their pretences are so gross that none can be sufferers in this respect, if they have not justly deserved it.

The reader may then rest assured that this process is not expensive, and reject all authors or practitioners who advance anything contrary to this established verity, remembering the simplicity of Nature in her operations, observing her frugal method in the production, and consummate wisdom in the dissolution of things; always endeavouring at something perfect in a new production. And because we are here proposing to help her in a metallic process, as before in the vegetable, let us consider a little how she forms the metals, in what state she has left them, and what need there is of the artist's skill to assist her in pushing them to that degree of perfection they are capable of attaining.

All true philosophers agree that the First Matter of metals is a moist vapour, raised by the action of the central fire in the bowels of the earth, which, circulating through its pores, meets with the crude air, and is coagulated by it into an unctuous water, adhering to the earth, which serves it for a receptacle, where it is joined to a sulphur more or less pure, and a salt more or less fixing, which it attracts from the air, and, receiving a certain degree of concoction from the central and solar heat, is formed into stones and rocks, minerals and metals. These were all formed of the same moist vapour originally, but are thus varied from the different impregnations of the sperm, the quality of salt and sulphur with which it is fixed, and the purity of the earth which serves it for a matrix; for whatever portion of this moist vapour is hastily sublimed to the surface of the earth, taking along its impurities, is soon deprived of its purer parts by the constant action of heat, both solar and central, and the grosser parts, forming a mucilaginous substance, furnish the matter of common rocks and stones. But when this moist vapour is sublimed, very slowly, through a fine earth, not partaking of a sulphureous unctuosity, pebbles are formed; for the sperm of these beautiful, variegated stones, with marbles, alabasters, etc., separates this depurated vapour, both for their first formation and continual growth. Gems are in like manner formed of this moist vapour when it meets with pure salt water, with which it is fixed in a cold place. But if it is sublimed leisurely through places which are hot and pure, where the fatness of sulphur adheres to it, this vapour, which the philosophers call their Mercury, is joined to that fatness and becomes an unctuous matter, which coming afterwards to other places, cleansed by the aforenamed vapours, where the earth is subtle, pure, and moist, fills the pores of it, and so gold is made. But if the unctuous matter comes into places cold and impure, lead, or Saturn, is produced; if the earth be cold and pure, mixed with sulphur, the result is copper. Silver also is formed of this vapour, where it abounds in purity, but mixed with a lesser degree of sulphur and not sufficiently concocted. In tin, or Jupiter, as it is called, it abounds, but in less purity. In Mars, or iron, it is in a lesser proportion impure, and mixed with an adust sulphur.

Hence it appears that the First Matter of metals is one thing, and not many, homogeneous, but altered by the diversity of places and sulphurs with which it is combined. The philosophers frequently describe this matter. Sendivogius calls it heavenly water, not wetting the hands; not vulgar, but almost like rain water. When Hermes calls it a bird without wings, figuring thereby its vaporous nature, it is well described. When he calls the sun its father and the moon its mother, he signifies that it is produced by the action of heat upon moisture. When he says the wind carries it in its belly, he only means that the air is its receptacle. When he affirms that which is inferior is like that which is superior, he teaches that the same vapour on the surface of the earth furnishes the matter of rain and dew, wherewith all things are nourished in the vegetable and animal kingdoms. This now is what the philosophers call their Mercury and affirm it to be found in all things, as it is in fact. This makes some suppose it to be in the human body, others in the dunghill, which has often bewildered such as are fond of philosophical subtleties, and fly from one thing to another, without any fixed theory about what they would seek, expecting to find in the Vegetable or Animal Kingdoms the utmost perfection of the Mineral. To this mistake of theirs, without doubt, the philosophers have contributed with an intention of hiding their First Matter from the unworthy; in which they were, perhaps, more cautious than is necessary, for Sendivogius declares that occasionally, in discourse, he had intimated the art plainly word by word to some who accounted themselves very acute philosophers; but they conceived such subtle notions, far beyond the simplicity of Nature, that they could not, to any purpose, understand his meaning. Wherefore he professes little fear of its being discovered but to those who have it according to the good pleasure and providence of the Most High.

  This benevolent disposition has induced him to declare more openly the First Matter, and fix the artist in his search of it to the mineral kingdom; for, quoting Albertus Magnus, who wrote that, in his time, grains of gold were found betwixt the teeth of a dead man in his grave, he observes that Albertus could not account for this miracle, but judged it to be by reason of the mineral virtue in man, being confirmed by that saying of Morien: "And this matter, O King, is extracted from thee." But this is erroneous, for Morien understood those things philosophically, the mineral virtue residing in its own kingdom, distinct from the animal. It is true, indeed, in the, animal kingdom mercury, or humidity, is as the matter, and sulphur, or marrow in the bones, as the virtue; but the animal is not mineral, and *vice versâ*. If the virtue of the animal sulphur were not in man, the blood, or mercury, could not be coagulated into flesh and bones; so if there were not a vegetable sulphur In the vegetable kingdom, it could not coagulate water, or the vegetable mercury, into herbs, etc. The same is to be understood in the mineral kingdom.

These three kingdoms do not, indeed, differ in their virtue, nor the three sulphurs, as every sulphur has a power to coagulate its own mercury; and every mercury has a power of being coagulated by its own proper sulphur, and by no other which is a stranger to it.

Now the reason why gold was found betwixt the teeth of a dead man is this: because in his lifetime mercury had been administered to him, either by unction, turbith, or some other way; and it is the nature of this metal to ascend to the mouth, forming itself an outlet there, to be evacuated with the spittle. If, then, in the time of such treatment, the sick man died, the mercury, not finding an egress, remained in his mouth between his teeth, and the carcase becoming a natural matrix to ripen the mercury, it was shut up for a long time, till it was congealed into gold by its own proper sulphur, being purified by the natural heat of putrefaction, caused by the corrosive phlegm of man's body; but this would never have happened if mineral mercury had not been administered to him.

CHAPTER V.
Of the Second Matter, or Seed in Metals.

ALL philosophers affirm, with one consent, that metals have a seed by which they are increased, and that this seminal quality is the same in all of them; but it is perfectly ripened in gold only, where the bond of union is so fixed that it is most difficult to decompound the subject, and procure it for the Philosophical Work. But some, who were adepts in the art, have by painful processes taken gold for their male, and the mercury, which they knew how to rextact from the less compacted metals, for a female: not as an easier process, but to find out the possibility of making the stone this way; and have succeeded, giving this method more openly to conceal the true confection, which is most easy and simple. We shall, therefore, set before the reader a landmark, to keep him from splitting on this difficulty, by considering what is the seed wherein the metals are increased, that the artist may be no longer at a loss where to seek for it, keeping in view the writings of our learned predecessors on this subject.

The seed of metals is what the Sons of Wisdom have called their mercury, to distinguish it from quicksilver, which it nearly resembles, being the radical moisture of metals. This, when judiciously extracted, without corrosives, or fluxing, contains in it a seminal quality whose perfect ripeness is only in gold; in the other metals it is crude, like fruits which are yet green, not being sufficiently digested by the heat of the sun and action of the elements. We observed that the radical moisture contains the seed, which is true: yet it is not the seed, but the sperm only, in which the vital principle floats, being invisible to the eye. But the mind perceives it, in a true artist, as a central point of condensed air, wherein Nature, according to the will of God, has included the first principles of life in everything, as well animal and vegetable as mineral; for in animals the sperm may be seen, but not the included principle of impregnation: this is a concentered point, to which the sperm serves only as a vehicle, till, by the action and ferment of the matrix, the point wherein Nature has included a vital principle expands itself, and then it is perceivable in the rudiments of an animal. So in any esculent fruit (as, for instance, in an apple), the pulp or sperm is much more in proportion than the seed included; and even that which appears to be seed is only a finer concoction of sperm, including the vital stamina; as also in a grain of wheat, the flour is only the sperm, the point of vegetation is an included air. which is kept by its sperm from the extremes of cold and heat, till it finds a proper matrix, where the husk being softened with moisture, and warmed by the heat, the surrounding sperm putrefies, making the seed, or concentered air, to expand and to burst the husk, carrying along in its motion a milky substance, assimilated to itself from the putrefied sperm. This the condensing quality of the air includes in a film and hardens into a germ, all according to the purpose of Nature.

    If this whole process of Nature, most wonderful in her operations, was not constantly repeated before our eyes, the simple process of vegetation would be equally problematical with that of the philosophers; yet how can the metals increase, nay, how can anything be multiplied without seed? The true artists never pretended to multiply metals without it, and can it be denied that Nature still follows her first appointment? She always fructifies the seed when it is put into a proper matrix. Does not she obey an ingenious artist, who knows her operations, with her possibilities, and attempts nothing beyond them? A husbandman meliorates his ground with compost, burns the weeds, and makes use of other operations. He steeps his seed in various preparations, only taking care not to destroy its vital principle; indeed, it never comes into his head to roast it, or to boil it, in which he shows more knowledge of Nature than some would-be philosophers do. Nature, like a liberal mother, rewards him with a more plentiful harvest, in proportion as he has meliorated her seed and furnished a more suitable matrix for its increase.

The intelligent gardener goes farther; he knows how to shorten the process of vegetation, or retard it. He gathers roses, cuts salads, and pulls green peas in winter. Are the curious inclined to admire plants and fruits of other climates? He can produce them in his stoves to perfection. Nature follows his directions unconstrained, always willing to obtain her end, viz., the perfection of her offspring. Open your eyes here, ye studious searchers of Nature! Is she so liberal in her perishing productions, how much more in those which are permanent, and can subsist in the fire? Attend, then, to her operations; if you procure the metallic seed, and ripen that by art which she is many ages in perfecting, it cannot fail but she will reward you with an increase proportioned to the excellency of your subject.

The reader will be apt to exclaim here: "Very fine! All this is well; but how shall the seed of metals be procured, and whence comes it that so few know how to gather it?" To this it is answered that the philosophers have hitherto industriously kept that a profound secret; some out of a selfish disposition, though otherwise good men. Others, who wished only for worthy persons to whom they might impart it, could not write of it openly, because covetousness and vanity have been governing principles in the world; and, being wise men, they knew that it was not the will of the Most High to inflame and cherish such odious tempers, the genuine offspring of pride and self-love, but to banish them out of the earth, wherefore they have been withheld hitherto. But we, finding no restraint on our mind in that respect, shall declare what we know: and the rather because we judge the time is come to demolish the golden calf, so long had in veneration by all ranks of men, insomuch that worth is estimated by the money a man possesses; and such is the inequality of possessions that mankind are almost reducible to the rich, who are rioting in extravagance, and the poor, who are in extreme want, smarting under the iron hand of oppression. Now the measure of iniquity among the rich hastens to its limit, and the cry of the poor is come before the Lord: "*Who will give them to eat till they shall be satisfied?*" Hereafter the rich will see the vanity of their possessions when compared with the treasures communicated by this secret; for the riches it bestows are a blessing from God, and not the squeezing of oppression. Besides, its chief excellence consists in making a medicine capable of healing all diseases to which the human body is liable, and prolonging life to the utmost limits ordained by the Creator of all things.

    There want not other reasons for the manifestation of the process; for scepticism has gone hand in hand with luxury and oppression, insomuch that the fundamental truths of all revealed religion are disputed. These were always held in veneration by the possessors of this art, as may be seen from what they have left upon record in their books: and, indeed, the first principles of revealed religion are demonstrated from the whole process, for the seed of metals is sown in corruption, and raised in incorruption; it is sown a natural body, and raised a spiritual body; it is known to partake of the curse which came upon the earth for man's sake, having in its composition a deadly poison, which can only be separated by a regeneration in water and fire; it can, when it is throughly purified and exalted, immediately tinge imperfect metals and raise them to a state of perfection, being in this respect a lively emblem of that seed of the woman, the Serpent Bruiser, who, through His sufferings and death, bath entered into glory, having thenceforth power and authority to redeem, purify, and glorify all those who come unto Him as a mediator between God and mankind.

  Such being our motives, we can no longer be silent concerning the seed of metals, but declare that it is contained in the ores of metals, as wheat is in the grain; and the sottish folly of alchemists has hindered them from adverting to this, so that they have always sought it in the vulgar metals, which are factitious and not a natural production, herein acting as foolishly as if a man should sow bread and expect corn from it, or from an egg which is boiled hope to produce a chicken. Nay, though the philosophers have said many times the vulgar metals are dead, not excepting gold, which passes the fire, they could never imagine a thing so simple as that the seed of metals was contained in their ores, where alone it ought to be expected; so bewildered is human ingenuity, when it leaves the beaten track of truth and Nature, to entangle itself in a multiplicity of fine-spun inventions.

The searcher of Nature will rejoice greatly in this discovery, as grounded in reason and sound philosophy; but to fools it would be in vain, should even Wisdom herself cry out in the streets. Wherefore, leaving such persons to hug themselves in their own imaginary importance, we shall go on to observe that the ores of metals are our First Matter, or sperm, wherein the seed is contained, and the key of this art consists in a right dissolution of the ores into a water, which the philosophers call their mercury, or water of life, and an earthy substance, which they have denominated their sulphur. The first is called their woman, wife, Luna, and other names, signifying that it is the feminine quality in their seed; the other they have denominated their man, husband, Sol, etc., to point out its masculine quality. In the separation and due conjunction of these with heat, and careful management, there is generated a noble offspring, which they have for its excellency called the quintessence, or a subject wherein the four elements are so completely harmonised as to produce a fifth subsisting in the fire, without waste of substance, or diminution of its virtue, wherefore they have given it the titles of Salamander, Phoenix, and Son of the Sun.

CHAPTER VI.
Of the Dissolution and Extraction of the Seed in Metals.

THE true Sons of Science have always accounted the dissolution of metals as the master key to this art, and have been particular in giving directions concerning it, only keeping their readers in the dark as to the subject, whether ores, or factitious metals, were to be chosen; nay, when they say most to the purpose, then they make mention of metals rather than the ores, with an intention to perplex those whom they thought unworthy of the art. Thus the author of the "Philosophical Duel," or a dialogue between the stone, gold, and mercury, says:

"By the omnipotent God, and on the salvation of my soul, I here declare to you earnest seekers, in pity to your earnest searching, the whole Philosophical Work, which is only taken from one subject and perfected in one thing. For we take this copper, and destroy its crude and gross body; we draw out its pure spirit, and after we have purified the earthy parts, we join them together, thus making a Medicine of a Poison.

It is remarkable that he avoids mentioning the ore, but calls his subject copper, which is what they call a metal of the vulgar, being indeed factitious, and not fit for the confection of our Stone, having lost its seminal quality in the fire; but in other respects it is the plainest discovery extant, and is accounted to be so by Sendivogius.

    Yet the reader is not to suppose that the ore of copper is to be chosen in consequence of that assertion, as preferable to others; no, the mercury, which is the metallic seed, is attainable from all, and is easier to be extracted from lead, which is confirmed by the true adepts, advising us to seek for the noble child where it lies in a despised form, shut up under the seal of Saturn; and, indeed, let it be supposed, for an illustration of this subject, that any one would propose to make malt, he may effect his purpose in the other corns, but barley is generally chosen, because its germ is made to sprout by a less tedious process, which is to all intents and purposes what we want in the extraction of our mercury: neither are the proceedings un-similar in both cases, if regard is had to the fixity of ores, and the ease with which barley gives forth its seminal virtue from the slight cohesion of its parts.

    Let the artist remark how a maltster manages his grain by wetting, to loosen the cohesion of its parts, and leaves the rest to Nature, knowing that she will soon furnish the necessary heat for his purpose, if he does not suffer it to escape by mismanagement in the laying of his heap too thin, or raising the fermentation too high by a contrary proceeding, as it is well known actual fire may be kindled from the fermentation of vegetable juices when crude; and ripe corn, under such treatment, would soon be fit for nothing but hogs, or the dunghill. Now the intention is to raise such a fermentation only as will draw out the vegetable mercury without spoiling it, either for the earth, if it was cast there to fructify, or the kiln, if it is to be fixed at that precise point, by exhaling the adventitious moisture, and thus preserving the whole strength of its seminal quality for the purposes of brewing, or making malt spirits.

    Suppose, then, an artist would extract a mineral mercury from the ores, and chooses lead ore for his subject. He can only assist Nature in the process by stirring up a central heat, which she includes in everything not already putrefied, as a root of its life, in which it is increased. The medium by which this central heat is put in motion is known to be putrefaction; but the ores of every kind are found to resist putrefaction in all known processes extant. They may, indeed, when they have been fluxed in the fire, contract a rust from the air, which is a gradual decomposition of their substance, but this is only the natural decay of a dead body, not the putrefaction of its sperm for the purposes of propagation; and we are sensible from the heat of furnaces which is required to flux the ores, and the slowness of their decay when deprived of their seminal qualities, by fluxation, that a heat which would destroy the seed in vegetables may be necessary in the first stages of putrefaction for the ores, as they will bear a red fire without being fluxed or losing anything but their sulphureous and arsenical impurities; in short, a matter in itself as much extraneous to the seed of metals, as the chaff to the wheat; wherefore, a careful separation of these by roasting, or otherwise, is deservedly reckoned among the first operations for the putrefaction of ores, and the rather because that which has been calcined, by having its pores opened, is rendered attractive, both of the air and other menstruums proper for its decomposition.

    Let the artist, therefore, by fire and manual operation, separate the impure qualities from his subject, pounding, washing, and calcining till no more blackness is communicated to his menstruum, for which pure rain water is sufficient. It will be seen on every repetition of this process, that what fouls the water is extraneous, and the ore yet exists in its individual metallic nature, except it is fluxed by a too intense heat, in which case it is no longer fit for our purpose; therefore fresh ore is to be used.

    The matter being thus prepared, its central fire will be awakened, if it is treated properly, according to the process for extracting quicksilver from it ores, by keeping it in a close heat, which is continued without admission of the crude air, till the radical moisture is elevated in the form of a vapour, and again condensed into a metallic water, analogous to quicksilver. This is the true mercury of the Philosophers, and fit for all their operations in the Hermetic Art.

CHAPTER VII.

Of the Separation and Further Treatment of our Philosophical Seed.

THE putrefaction of our subject being thus completed, it exists under two forms: the moisture which was extracted, and the residuum, being our Philosophical Earth and Water. The water contains its seminal virtue, and the earth is a proper receptacle, wherein it may fructify. Let the water, then be separated and kept for use; calcine tile earth, for an impurity adheres to it which can only be taken away by fire, and that, too, of the strongest degree: for here there is no danger of destroying the seminal quality, and our earth must be highly purified before it can ripen the seed. This is what Sendivogius means when he says: *Burn the sulphur till it becomes sulphur incombustible. Many lose in the preparation what is of most use in the art; for our mercury is acuated by the sulphur, else it would be of no use.* Let, therefore, the earthy part be well calcined, and return the mercury on the calcined earth; afterwards draw it off by distillation; then calcine, cohobate, and distil, repeating the process till the mercury is well acuated by the sulphur, and the sulphur is purified to a whiteness, and goes on to red, a sign of its complete purification, where you have the Philosophical Male and Female ready for conjunction. This must now be managed with judgment, as the noble child may be yet strangled in the birth; but all things are easy to an ingenious artist, who knows the proportion of mixture required and accommodates his operations to the intentions of Nature, for which purpose we shall faithfully conduct him according to our ability.

CHAPTER VIII.
Of the Union or Mystical Marriage in the Philosophical Process.

THE seed and its earth being thus prepared, nothing remains but a judicious conjunction of them together; for if too much moisture prevails, the philosophical egg may be burst before it can go through the heat necessary for its hatching. To speak without a figure. Our subject must now be enclosed in a small glass vial, made strong enough to bear a due heat, which is to be raised gradually to the highest degree: the best form for this vessel being that of an oil flask, with a long neck; but these are much too thin in substance for this operation. In such a vessel the mixture is to be sealed hermetically, and digested so long till it is fixed into a dry concretion; but, if, as we observed, the moisture should predominate, there is great danger of the vessel bursting, with a vapour which cannot be concentered by the fixing quality in the matter. The intention is, nevertheless, to fix our subject in the heat, and so render its future destruction impossible.

On the other hand, if the dry, fixing quality of the sulphur exceeds so as not to suffer an alternate resolution of its substance into vapours, and a re-manifestation of its fixing quality, by causing the whole to subside in the bottom of the vessel till the matter again liquefies and sublimes (which Ripley has well described), there is danger of the whole vitrifying; and thus you shall have only glass instead of the noble tincture. To avoid these two extremes it is very proper that the purified earth be reduced by manual operation to an impalpable fineness, and then its acuated mercury must be added, incorporating both together till the earth will imbibe no more. This operation will require time, with some degree of the artist's patience; for however the humidity may seem disproportionate, on letting it rest awhile, a dryness on the surface of your matter will show that it is capable of imbibing more, so that the operation is to be repeated till it is fully saturated, which may be known from its bearing the air without any remarkable change of surface from dry to humid; or, on the contrary, if so, the conjunction is well made, which is farther confirmed if a small portion be spread upon a thin plate of iron, heated till it flows gently like wax, casting forth the moisture with heat and again absorbing it when cold, so as to return to the former consistence; but if a clamminess ensues it is a sign you have exceeded in the quantity of humidity, which must be extracted by distilling again and repeating the process till it is right.

Your sulphur and mercury being thus united, put them into a glass vial, before described, in such a quantity as to take up one-third of its contents, leaving two-thirds, including the neck, for the circulation of your matter. Secure the neck of your vial with a temporary luting at the first, and give a gentle heat, observing whether it sublimes and fixes alternately. If it easily sublimes and shows a disposition, at intervals, to subside at the bottom of the vessel, all is well conducted hitherto; for the moisture will first be predominant, which the sulphur can only perfectly absorb as the heat is increased for the perfect ripening of our

Paradisaical Fruit. Therefore, if it manifests a too early disposition for fixing, add more of the acuated mercury till Luna rises resplendent in her season; she will give place to the Sun in his turn. This would be the language of an adept on this occasion, only suggesting that the female quality in our prepared seed is first active, while the male is passive, and that it is afterwards passive while the male is active, such being the case in all vegetation; for every germ which is the first rudiments of a herb or tree, is predominant in moisture, and then only becomes fixed when it is fully concocted in the seed.

CHAPTER IX.
Of the Further Treatment and Ripening of our Seed.

THIS is deservedly called the Great Work of the Philosophers; and the artist having done his part hitherto, must seal up his glass hermetically, an operation which every maker of barometers knows how to perform.

The glass is then to be put into a furnace with a proper nest contrived for its reception, so as to give a continual heat from the first to the fourth degree, and to afford the artist an opportunity, from time to time, of inspecting every change which his matter assumes during the process, without danger of damping the heat and putting a stop to its perfect circulation. A heat of the first degree is sufficient at the first, for some months, in which method much time may be lost by a young practitioner, till he knows how to handle his matter from experience; but then he is not so liable to be disappointed with the bursting of his vessel or the matter vitrifying.

Thus you have arrived at the desired seed-time in our Philosophical Work, which, though it may appear in the artist's power to ripen, depends no less on the Divine blessing than the harvest, which a painful husbandman has not the presumption to expect otherwise than from God's beneficence.

There are many requisites to entitle anyone to the possession of our philosophical harvest, and the true labourers in it have sought for such persons to whom they might communicate it, by evident testimony of the senses, after which they account the confection of our Stone an easy process, manageable by women and children; but without such a communication, there is a necessity that those who would undertake it are endowed by Nature with an ingenious mind, patient to observe and accurate to investigate her ordinary appearances which, from their commonness, are less noticed than such phenomena as are more curious though of less importance; yet these for the most part employ the precious time of those egregious triflers, the modern virtuosi. These smatterers in philosophy are in raptures upon the discovery of a shell or butterfly differently streaked from those of the same kind: and all the while water, air, earth, fire, with their continual changes and resolutions into one another, by the medium of our atmosphere, through the efficacy of the central and solar heat, are unstudied by these would-be philosophers; so that a sensible rustic has more real knowledge, in this respect, than a collector of natural rarities, and makes a much wiser use of what experience he has acquired.

CHAPTER X.

Of the Further Process to the Ripening of our Noble Seed.

SUPPOSING such dispositions in the artist as have been previously laid down, and the work well performed hitherto, for his direction herein we shall describe the changes which our subject undergoes during the second part of the process, commonly called the Great Work of the Philosophers.

Our vessel being warily heated at the first for fear of its cracking, an ebullition of the contained matter is brought on, so that the moisture is alternately circulated in white fumes above, and condensed below, which may continue for a month or two, nay longer, increasing the heat gradually to another degree, as your matter discovers a disposition for fixing, by the vapour continuing at longer intervals condensed, and rising in a lesser quantity, of an ash colour, or other dark shades, which it will assume as a medium to perfect blackness, the first desirable stage in our harvest. Other colours may be exhibited in this part of the work without danger, if they pass transiently; but if a faint redness, like that of the corn poppy, continues, the matter is in danger of vitrifying, either from an impatient urging of the fire, or the moisture not being sufficiently predominant.

An ingenious artist can remedy this by opening his vessel and adding more of the acuated mercury, sealing it up as before; but a novice would do much better to prevent it by governing his fire according to the appearances of his matter, with judgment and patience, increasing it if the moisture manifests its predominancy too long, and slacking if the dry prevails, till such time as the vapours become dark; and after they have continued for some time at rest, a pellicle or film on the matter shows its disposition for fixing, retaining the vapour captive for some time, till it breaks through at different places on its surface (much like the bituminous substance of coal in a soldering fire), with darker clouds, but quickly dissipated, and growing less in quantity, till the whole substance resembles molten pitch, or the aforesaid bituminous substance, bubbling less and less, resting in one entire black substance at the bottom of your glass. This is called the blackness of black, the head of the crow, etc., and is esteemed a desirable stage in our philosophical generation, being the perfect putrefaction of our seed, which will ere long show its vital principle by a glorious manifestation of Seminal Virtue.

CHAPTER XI.
A Further Description of the Process.

WHEN the putrefaction of our seed has been thus completed, the fire may be increased till glorious colours appear, which the Sons of Art have called *Cauda Pavonis*, or the *Peacock's Tail*. These colours come and go, as heat is administered approaching to the third degree, till all is of a beautiful green, and as it ripens assumes a perfect whiteness, which is the White Tincture, transmuting the inferior metals into silver, and very powerful as a medicine. But as the artist well knows it is capable of a higher concoction; he goes on increasing his fire till it assumes a yellow, then an orange or citron colour; and then boldly gives a heat of the fourth degree, till it acquires a redness like blood taken from a sound person, which is a manifest sign of its thorough concoction and fitness for the uses intended.

CHAPTER XII.
Of the Stone and its Uses.

HAVING thus completed the operation, let the vessel cool, and on opening it you will perceive your matter to be fixed into a ponderous mass, thoroughly of a scarlet colour, which is easily reducible to powder by scraping, or otherwise, and in being heated in the fire flows like wax, without smoking, flaming, or loss of substance, returning when cold to its former fixity, heavier than gold, bulk for bulk, yet easy to be dissolved in any liquid, in which a few grains being taken its operation most wonderfully pervades the human body, to the extirpation of all disorders, prolonging life by its use to its utmost period; and hence it has obtained the apellation of "*Panacea*," or a Universal Remedy. Therefore, be thankful to the Most High for the possession of such an inestimable jewel, and account the possession of it not as the result of your own ingenuity, but a gift bestowed, of God's mere bounty, for the relief of human infirmities, in which your neighbour ought to share jointly with you, without any grudging or sinister views, according to the charge delivered to the Apostles, "Freely have you received, freely communicate," remembering at the same time not to cast your pearls before swine; in a word, to withhold the manifestations of Nature you are enabled to exhibit, by the possession of our Stone, from the vicious and unworthy.

CHAPTER XIII.

Of the Transmutation.

IT is much to be lamented that the seekers of natural knowledge in this art propose, principally, the Science of Transmutation as their ultimate view, and overlooking the chief excellency of our Stone as a medicine. Notwithstanding this grovelling spirit, we shall commit the issue to His Providence, and declare the Transmutation (which, indeed, the philosophers do) openly, after which we shall describe the further circulation of our Stone for an increase of its virtues, and then make an end of our treatise.

When the artist would transmute any metal—for instance, lead—let a quantity be melted in a clean crucible, to which let a few grains of gold in filings be cast; and when the whole is melted, let him have in readiness a little of the powder, which will easily scrape off from his "stone," the quantity inconsiderable, and cast it on the metal while in fusion. Immediately there will arise a thick fume, which carries off with it the impurities contained in the lead, with a crackling noise, and leaves the substance of the lead transmuted into most pure gold, without any kind of sophistication; the small quantity of gold added, previous to projection, serves only as a medium to facilitate the transmutation, and the quantity of your tincture is best ascertained by experience, as its virtue is proportioned to the number of circulations you have given after the first has been completed.

    For instance: when you have finished the stone, dissolve it in our mercury again, wherein you have previously dissolved a few grains of pure gold. This operation is done without trouble, both substances readily liquefying. Put it into your vessel, as before, and go through the process. There is no danger in the management, but breaking your vessel; and every time it is thus treated its virtues are increased, in a ratio of ten to one hundred, a thousand, ten thousand, etc., both in medicinal and transmuting qualities; so that a small quantity may suffice for the purposes of an artist during the remaining term of his life.

END.

THE BOSOM BOOK
OF
SIR GEORGE RIPLEY,

Canon of Bridlington:
CONTAINING
His Philosophical Accurtations in Making the Philosopher's Mercury and Elixirs.

THE BOSOM BOOK OF SIR GEORGE RIPLEY.

The whole work of the composition of the Philosophical Stone of the great elixir and of the first solution of the gross body.

FIRST take thirty pounds weight of sericon, or antimony, which will make twenty-one pounds weight of gum, or near thereabouts, if it be well dissolved and the vinegar is very good; and dissolve each pound thereof in a gallon of twice distilled vinegar. When cold again, and, as it standeth in dissolution in a fit glass vessel, stir it about with a clean stick very often every day, the oftener the better; and when it is well molten to the bottom, then filter over the said liquors three several times, which keep close covered, and cast away the fæces, for that is superfluous filth which must be removed and entereth not into the work, but is called *Terra damnata*.

The making of our Gum, or Green Lion.

Then put all these cold liquors, thus filled, into a fit glass vessel and set it in *Balneo Mariæ* to evaporate in a temperate heat; which done, our sericon will be coagulated into a green gum called our Green Lion; which gum dry well, yet beware thou burn not his flowers, nor destroy his greenness.

The extraction of our Menstruum or Blood of our Green Lion.

Then take out the said gum and put it into a strong retort of glass, very well luted, and place it in your furnace, and under that, at the first, make sober fire, and anon you see a white smoke or fume issue. Then put, too, a receiver of glass, which must have a very large belly and the mouth no wider than it may well receive into that the neck of the retort, which close well together, that no fume issue forth of the receiver. Then increase your fire by little and little, till the fume which issueth be reddish; then continue the greater fire, until drops like blood come forth, and no more fume will issue forth; and when that leaveth bleeding, let it cool, or assuage the fire by little and little; and when all things are cold then take away the receiver, and close it fast suddenly, that the spirits vanish not away, for this liquor is called our blessed liquor: which liquor keep close stopped in a glass till hereafter. Then look into the neck of the retort, and therein you will find a white hard rime, as it were the congelation of a frosty vapour, or much like sublimate, which gather with diligence and keep it apart, for therein are contained great secrets which shall be showed hereafter, after the great work is ended.

The Creation of our Basis.

Then take out all the fæces which remain in the retort, and are blackish like unto soot, which feces are called our Dragon, of which fæces calcine one pound or more at your pleasure in a fervent hot fire, in a potter's or glass-maker's furnace, or in a furnace of vent (or a wind furnace), until it become a white calx, as white as snow; which white calx keep well and clean by itself, for it is called the basis and foundation of the work, and is now called Mars, and our White Fixed Earth, or *Ferrum Philosophorum*.

The Calcination of the Black Fæces, called our Black Dragon.

Then take all the rest of the aforesaid black fæces, or Black Dragon, and spread them somewhat thin upon a clean marble, or other fit stone, and put into the one side thereof a burning coal, and the fire will glide through the fæces within half-an-hour, and calcine them into a citrine colour very glorious to behold.

The Solution of the said Fæces.

Then dissolve those citrine fæces in such distilled vinegar as you did before, and then filter it likewise three times as before, and after make or evaporate it into a gum again, and then draw out of it more of our menstruum, called now Dragon's Blood, and iterate this work in all points as afore until you have either brought all or the most part of the fæces into our natural and blessed liquor: all which liquor put to the first liquor or menstrue called the Green Lion's blood, and set that liquor altogether in one vessel of glass fourteen days in putrefication; and after proceed to the separation of elements, for now have you all the fire of the stone in this our blessed liquor, which before lay hidden in the fæces; which secret all the philosophers do marvellously hide.

The Separation of the Elements whereof the first is the Air, and is also counted our Ardent Water and our Water Attractive.

Then put all the said putrefied menstruum into a still of fine Venice glass, fit for the quantity thereof; put on the limbeck, and close it to the still with a fine linen cloth dipped in the white of an egg, and then set it in *Balneo Mariæ*, put to the receiver, which must be of great length, that the spirit respire not out again; and with a very temperate heat separate the elements one from another, and then the element of air will issue forth first, which is an oil.

Our Ardent Water or Water Attractive is thus made.

When all the first element is distilled, then in another still, fit for it, rectify it: that is to say, distil it over seven several times, and until it will burn a linen cloth clean up that is dipped into it, when it is put to the flame, which is then called our Ardent Water rectified and is also called our Water Attractive; which keep very close stopped, for otherwise the spirit thereof, which is very subtle, will vanish away. By often rectifying the ardent water, there will come air in a white oil swimming above the water, and there will remain behind a yellow oil, which with a stronger fire will also come over. Put sublimate, beaten small, upon a plate of iron, and in the cold it will dissolve into water, and will draw to itself all the mercury in the form of a green oil swimming aloft; which separate and put into a retort, and distil first a water, and afterward will come a green thick oil, which is the oil of mercury.

The Flood or Water of the Stone.

Then draw out the flood or water of the stone by itself in another receptory, which liquor will be somewhat white, and draw it with a very gentle fire of Balneum, until there remain in the bottom of the still a thick oily substance, like unto liquid pitch; keep this water by itself in a fit glass, very close stopped.

NOTE.—When the liquor cometh white you must put on another receiver, for then all that element is come over; two or three drops of this black liquid oil given in spirit of wine cureth all poison taken inwardly.

Our Man's Blood is thus taken and rectified.

Then put our ardent water upon that matter black and liquid; stir them well together, and let it so stand well covered for three hours; then decant and filter it; put on fresh ardent water, and repeat this operation three times, and then distil it again with a moist lent fire of Balneum;

and so do three times, and then it is called Man's Blood rectified, which the workers in the secrets of Nature do seek, and so thou hast the elements exalted in the virtue of their quintessence, namely, the flood that is water and the air. Let this blood be kept for a season.

The Oil or Fire, as the Earth of the Stone.

Then put up the flood, or water, upon the black and soft matter or earth of the stone; let them be well mingled together, and then distil the whole till there remain in the bottom an earth most dry and black, which is the earth of the stone; save the oil with the water for a season, close stopped in any wise.

The Fiery Water.

Then beat this black earth into powder, and mingle it with man's blood, and so let it stand three hours; after that distil it on ashes with a good fire, and reiterate this work three times; and then it shall be water of the fire rectified, and so hast thou three of the elements exalted into the virtue of the quintessence, namely water, air, and fire.

The Earth.

Then calcine the earth black and dry in a furnace of reverberation, until it become a very fine white calx.

The Water of Life, which is our Mercury and our Lunary.

Then mingle with this white calx the fiery water, and distil it with a strong fire all off as before, and calcine the earth again that remaineth in the bottom of the still, and then distil it again with a strong fire as before, and again calcine it, and thus distil and calcine it seven times, until all the substance of the calx be lifted up by the limbec: and then thou hast the water of life rectified and made indeed spiritual; and so hast thou the four elements exalted in the virtue of their quintessence. This water will dissolve all bodies, and putrefy them, and purge them: and this is our Mercury and our Lunary; and whosoever thinketh there is any other water than this is an ignorant and a fool, and shall never be able to come to the effect.

Ripley's .Secret Accurtation for the help of those who have the Philosopher's Mercury, and are unable to proceed to either the Red or White Elixir.

    Take the cerus, or cream, of the finest and purest Cornish tin molten, reduce it into fine white calx, put it into a fit glass still, and there upon pour a convenient quantity of our, when it is our Lunary perfect; then distil that mercury from the calx again; imbibe it again therewith, and again distil; reiterate this work until the calx is become subtle and oily, yea, so subtle indeed that it will flow upon a plate of copper, fiery hot as wax, and not evaporate, which then will convert copper into fine silver, for the softness and neshness of the tin is taken away by the benefit of our ☿, confixed unto it, by the virtue of which it is made indurate and clean, that it may agree with hard bodies in fusion and in malleation, even as pure silver. This work is very gainful and easy to be dealt withal; use it therefore until thou be rich, and then, I pray thee, for Our Lord's sake, go to the great work, which is here truly set forth unto thee, according as by practice I have wrought and proved the same. For the which thank God.

The Oil which is the Element of Fire and our Red Mercury.

The flood, with the oil afore reserved, shall be distilled with a most lent fire *in Balneo*, and the red oil which remaineth in the bottom shall be diligently kept by itself, for it is the Element of Fire; the water shall be rectified again, and the same work iterated, until no more of our said red Lunary will remain in it.

The Work of Putrefication.

When all your Elements be thus separated, then take the white calcined *Fæces* first of all reserved, called *Mars*, and put so much thereof into a chymia as will scarcely fill half the glass, and thereupon pour so much of our Ardent Water rectified as may but well cover the *calx*; which done, incontinent stop close the glass with a blind head, and set it into a cold place, until the calx have drunk up all the liquor, which it will do in eight days. Then imbibe it again with the like quantity of the same water, and let it stand eight days more, and so reiterate the work, from eight days to eight days, until the same calx will drink no more, but stand liquid still; then seal up the glass with Hermes' seal and set it in *Balneo Mariæ* in a temperate heat to putrefaction.

The Digestion of the White Stone.

Then in that temperate *Balneum* let your glass stand unremoved by the space of fully 150 days, and until the stone within the glass become first russet and after whitish green, and after that very white, like unto the eyes of fishes, which then is Sulphur of Nature flowing, and not evaporating in fire, and our white stone ready to be fermented.

Another Secret Accurtation of Sir George Ripley.

Take the above said Sulphur of Nature, and project a quantity upon a plate of glass fiery hot, and the glass shall be converted into a silver colour, and that colour shall not be removed by any art.

The Digestion of the Red Stone.

Then take out the white stone and divide it into two, and know the true weight of each half: the one half reserve to the white work, the other half put into the glass, and seal it up again with Hermes' seal, and then remove the glass into a cinerition, which is somewhat a hotter fire, and let it stand there likewise unremoved in that digestion, until it become red, and of a purple colour, so have you the red stone also ready to be fermented.

The Preparation of the Ferment to the White Stone.

Then take silver, well purged from all metals and other filth that may be joined with it, and dissolve it in as much of our Lunary, which is our ☿ as the quantity of your silver is (and in no greater quantity, as near as you may), and set it upon warm ashes close covered, and when it is throughly dissolved, the whole liquor will be green; then rectify our ☿ clean from it again twice or thrice, so that no drop of our ☿ be left with it, then seal up the oil of *Luna* in a *Chemia*, and set it in *Balneo* to putrefy until it show all colours, and at the last come to be crystalline white, which then is the white Ferment of Ferments.

The Fermentation of the White Stone.

Then put that half of the white stone, before reserved, for the white work into a fit glass, and know his weight, and put so much of the foresaid Lune ferment into the glass with the stone as may contain the fourth part of the said stone; and in the said glass, well kited, fix them together, in a fixatory vessel under the fire, which will be well done in two or three days.

The Inceration of the White Stone.

When they are thus fixed together, and become one very fine powder, incerate, that is to say, imbibe it with the white oil of our stone, which is our Lunary, by pouring on, as it were, drop after drop, until the stone be oilish; then congeal it, and again imbibe it, and in this manner iterate this work, until this stone will flow in fire like wax, when it is put upon a plate of copper fiery hot, and not evaporate, and congeal it up until it be hard, white, and transparent clear as crystal; then it is the Medicine of the Third Degree, and the Perfect White Stone, transmuting all metalline bodies, and chiefly copper and iron, into pure and perfect silver.

The Preparation of the Red Ferment.

Then likewise take gold, very purely first purged from all other metals that may be joined with it, with ten parts of antimony, and then dissolve it in our, or liquor solutive, as before you did the Lune; and when it is perfectly dissolved the liquor will be citrine; then, in like manner rectify from it again our ☿, or liquor solutive, and then seal up the oil of Gold Ferment in a *Chemia* fit for it, and set it in *Balneo* to putrefy, which likewise will become black, and must stand still unremoved in digestion, until it become white, which then remove into a stronger fire, without opening the glass, and then keep it until it change colours and become citrine, which then is also Ferment of Ferments for the Red Work.

The Fermentation of the Red Stone.

Then to the other half of the stone before rubefied, digested, and reserved for the Red Work, put so much of the foresaid Gold Ferment as may contain the fourth part of the said stone; and then fix them as you did the white stone, under fire in a fixatory vessel, which will be then very well done in two or three days.

The Work of Inceration for the Red.

When they are thus fixed together, and thereby become one very fine powder, incerate, that is imbibe it, with the Red Oil of our stone; then congeal it again, and again imbibe and congeal, and iterate this work so often until it will flow in fire as wax, but not evaporate when it is put upon a plate of copper fiery hot; which then congeal up until it be clear, transparent, hard, red in colour, like a ruby or jacinth, which then is the Medicine of the Third Degree, and the Perfect Red Stone, transmuting all bodies, and especially ☿, ♄, and ☽ into as pure ☉ as any of the natural mine.

Thus have you the making of the Philosopher's Stones, both white and red, which is the Great Secret of Philosophers. These stones must be kept by themselves, in several glasses, or fair boxes, in a warm place, or dry at the least, as you would keep sugar, because they are of so tender and oily substance, as they are apt to dissolve in every moist place, which therefore preserve as is here showed.

The Multiplication or Increase of the Virtue and Goodness of the aforesaid White and Red Stone.

If you list to exalt your medicine, or stone, in quantity or goodness, then put your aforesaid white or red stone, or part of each, into a several vial of glass fit for the quantity; close well the vial, then hang your glass or glasses in *Balneo Mariæ vaporoso*, so that it touch not the water; in this warm fume or breath, the stone, which was congealed before in the glass, will now be dissolved, which then congeal again upon warm ashes, and again thus dissolve and congeal, and so iterate this work of dissolution and congelation until at last the stone within the glass dissolved will be congealed, as soon as he cometh out of the pot or Balneum, and feeleth the cold air, without any other manner of congelation to be used: and note that how often in this work you dissolve and congeal your said medicine or stone, so many times doth he increase his virtue ten times in projection; so that if at the first one ounce will convert one hundred ounces, after the second solution the same one shall convert one thousand, after the third ten thousand, after the fourth one hundred thousand, and after the fifth one million parts of any imperfect metal into pure and true gold and silver, in all examinations, as any of the natural mine.

The Way of Projection.

Because it is very cumbersome to melt a thousand thousand parts of any body, when you will make projection thus do:

Take one hundred ounces of ☿ first washed with salt and vinegar, and put it into a crucible, and set it over the fire; and when that cloth begin to wax hot, put in one ounce of your elixir, or medicine, thus prepared as afore taught you, upon those one hundred parts of the cleansed ☿ and all the said ☿ shall become medicine; project one ounce of that medicine upon another hundred ounces, of other washed ☿ and it shall all also be converted into medicine. Again the third time project one ounce of this congealed ☿ upon another hundred ounces of washed ☿ and all shall be converted into medicine; then project, the fourth time, one ounce of this, last congealed ☿ upon another hundred ounces of other washed ☿ and all that shall be converted into gold or silver, according as your stone was prepared, to the white or red. Praised be God.

Accurtation of the Great Work which saveth half the Work and Labour in the Work revealed by Sir George Ripley

The white frosty rime, or powder, whereof I told you in the beginning, being found in the neck of the retort, after the drawing of the menstruum, is like sublimate, and is perfect Sulphur of Nature, and therefore needeth neither putrefaction nor digestion into white. Of this sulphur take either the half, or the whole if you list, and also take so much of Lune Ferment, when it is Ferment of Ferments, as may contain the fourth part of the said Sulphur. Seal them up both together in a chemia, and fix them together under the fire in a fixatory vessel, which will be well done in three days; and when they are become one very fine white powder, then incerate, that is to say, imbibe it, with the White Oil of our Stone, which is our ☿congealed; and imbibe and iterate this work, and in all points do as you did in the white work, in the great *Elixir* before; for this sulphur is of the sane nature, and thus shall you have the white work perfectly made, and the Stone, in half the time, and with half the labour, which is not only a precious jewel, but a great secret also.

The like Accurtation of the Red Work done by the aforesaid Sulphur.

Take either the one half or the whole of this above said Sulphur of Nature, and dissolve it once with our red Mercury. Congeal it again, and then seal it up in a *Chemia* and set it in cinerition (or ashes) till it be throughly digested, and until it hath put on the Purple Colour or Fiery Chariot. Then put thereunto so much of the Ferment of *Sol*, when it is Ferment of Ferments, as may contain the fourth part of the said sulphur; then fix them together under a fire in a fixatory vessel, which will be well done in three days, and when they become one very fine Red Powder, then increate that is, imbibe it with the red oil of our stone, which is our Red and Red Lunary, and Fire of the Stone, and continue in doing in all points as in the great work aforesaid until the stone be hard, transparent, in colour like a ruby or jacinth flowing in fire, and not evaporating; then have you, with less labour and expense of time, the perfect Red Stone, for which thank God.

This is the pleasant and dainty Garden of the Philosophers, which beareth the sweet smelling roses white and red, abbreviated out of all the Work of the Philosophers, containing in it nothing superfluous or

diminished, teaching to make infinitely gold and silver according as the medicine was prepared, having virtue to heal all griefs and sicknesses, as well proceeding of cold as of hot causes, through the subtlety of its nature, above all other medicines of physicians: for it comforteth the healthy, strengtheneth the weak, and maketh the aged seem young, and driveth away all grief, and putteth venom from the heart; it moisteneth the arteries and joints; it dissolveth all things in the lungs; it cleanseth the blood; it purgeth the pipes, and keepeth them clean; and if the sickness be of one month's continuance, it healeth it in one day, if of one year's continuance, it healeth it in twelve days, and if the grief be very old, it healeth it in one month. To conclude, whosoever hath this medicine, he hath an incomparable medicine above all treasures of the world. Praise God.
            FINIS.

PREPARATIONS
OF THE
SOPHIC MERCURY.

EXPERIMENTS
FOR THE PREPARATION OF THE SOPHIC
MERCURY, BY LUNA AND THE ANTIMONIAL
STELLATE REGULUS OF MARS, FOR THE
PHILOSOPHERS STONE.

Written by *Eirenæus Philalethes*, an Englishman, and a Cosmopolite.

THE SOPHIC MERCURY.

1. *The Secret of the Philosophic Arsenic.*

I took one part of the Fiery Dragon, and of the Magnetical Body two parts; I prepared them together by a strong fire, and in the first fusion there was made about eight ounces of the true arsenic.

2. *The Secret of Prepaying the Mercury with his Arsenic for the Separating its Fæces.*

I did take one part of the best arsenic, and I made a marriage with two parts of the Virgin *Diana* into one body; I ground it very fine, and with this I have prepared my Mercury, working them altogether in heat, until that they were most exquisitely incorporated; then I purged it with the salt of urine, that the fæces did separate, which I put away.

3. *The Purification of the Sophic Mercury.*

The Mercury, thus prepared, is yet infected with an external uncleanness, wherefore distil it three or four times in its proper alembic, with its steel cucurbit; then wash it with the salt of urine until that it be clear and bright, and in its motion leaves no tail behind it.

4. Another most excellent Purgation.

Take of decrepit salt, and of the Scoriæ of Mars, of each ten ounces, of prepared Mercury one ounce and a-half; grind the salt and the Scoriæ very fine together, in a marble mortar; then put in the Mercury, and grind it with vinegar, so long until no more of the Mercury appears. Put it into a glass body, and distil it by sand in a glass alembic, until all the Mercury be ascended pure, clear, and splendidly bright; reiterate this three times, and you will have the Mercury excellently well prepared for the Magistery.

5. The Secret of the just Preparation of the Sophic Mercury.

Every single preparation of the Mercury with its arsenic is one Eagle; the Feathers of the Eagle being purged from their crow-like blackness, make it to fly the seventh flight, and it is prepared even until the tenth flight.

6. The Secret of the Sophie Mercury.

I have taken the proper quantity of the ☿ and I mixed it with its true arsenic, to wit, about four ounces of Mercury, and I made a thin commixed consistence; I purged it after a due manner, and I distilled it, and I had a pure body of Lune, whence I knew that I had rightly prepared it. Afterwards I added to its weight of arsenic, and I increased its former weight of Mercury, in so much that the Mercury might prevail to a thin flux, and so I purged it, to the washing of the blackness almost to a lunary whiteness. Then I took half an ounce of the arsenic, of which I made a due marriage; I added it to this betrothed Mercury, and there was made a temperature like potter's loam, but a little thinner; I purged it again, after a due manner; the purgation was laborious, and a long time. I made it with the salt of urine which I have found to be the best in this work.

7. *Another Purgation, but yet better.*

I have found out a better way of purging it, with vinegar and pure sea salt, so that in the space of half-a-day I can prepare one Eagle: I made the first Eagle to fly, and Diana is left, with a little tincture of brass. I began the second Eagle by removing the superfluities, and then I made it fly, and again the Doves of Diana are left, with the tincture of brass. I conjoined the third Eagle, and I purged the superfluities, by removing them, even to a whiteness; then I made it fly, and there was left a great part of brass, with the Doves of Diana. Then I made it fly twice by itself, to the whole extraction of all the body. Then I joined the fourth Eagle, by adding more and more of its own humour by degrees, and there was made a very temperate consistence, in which there was no Hydrops (or superfluous moisture) as there was in the former Eagles.

8. *I have found the best way of Preparing the Sophie Mercury, viz., such as follows:*

The amalgamated mass, espoused or joined very intimately by a due marriage, I put into a crucible, and into a furnace of sand for half-an-hour, but so that it may not sublime; then I take it out, and strongly grind it; then I put it again in a crucible, and in the furnace, and after a quarter of an hour, or thereabouts, I grind it again, and I make the mortar hot. By this means the amalgam begins to be clean, and to cast forth a great deal of powder. Then I put it in the crucible again, and to the fire as before, for a convenient time, so that it be not sublimed: otherwise the greater the fire is, the better it is; so continually putting it in the tire, and continually grinding it, till almost all the powder Both wholly disappear; then I wash it, and the fæces are easily cast out, and the amalgam becomes entire without any heterogeneity. Then I wash it with salt, and again do heat it and grind it. This I repeat to the full, cleansing it from all manner of fæces.

9. *A Threefold Trial of the Goodness of the Prepared Mercury.*

Take thy Mercury prepared with its arsenic of seven, eight, nine, or ten Eagles; put it into a phial, and thou shalt lute it with the *Lutum Sapientiæ*. Place it in a furnace of sand, and let it stand in a heat of sublimation, so that it may ascend and descend in the glass, until it be coagulated a little thicker than butter. Continue it unto a perfect coagulation, until it be as white as silver.

10. *Another Trial.*

If by shaking it in a glass with the salt of urine, it be turned into an impalpable white powder of its own accord, so that it doth not appear as Mercury, and of its own accord, in a hot and dry place, it coagulates again into a thin Mercury, it is enough: but yet better if being agitated in fountain water, it runs into small heads or particles; for if the grain be in the body it will not be thus converted and separated into small minute parts.

11. *The Third Trial.*

Distil it in a glass alembic, from a glass cucurbit; if it passes over and leaves nothing behind it, it is a good mineral water.

12. *The Extraction of the Sulphur from the living Mercury by Separation.*

Take thy mixed corporal and spiritual compound, the body of which is coagulated of the volatile by digestion, and separate the Mercury from its Sulphur by a glass still, and thou shalt have a white *Luna* fixed and resisting *Aqua fortis*, and more ponderous than common silver.

13. *The Magical Sol out of this Luna.*

Out of this white Sulphur, by fire, thou shalt have a yellow Sulphur, by a manual operation, which Sol is the Red Lead of the Philosophers.

14. *Out of this Sulphur, Aurum Potabile.*

Thou mayst turn this yellow Sulphur into an oil as red as blood, by circulating it with the Volatile-Mercurial-Philosophical Menstruum; so thou shalt have an admirable panacea, or universal medicine.

15. *The Gross Conjunction of the Menstruum with its Sulphur, for the Formation of the Offspring of the Fire.*

Take of thy purged, best, prepared, and choicest Mercury, of seven, eight, nine, or at most ten Eagles; mix it with the prepared Laton, or its Red Sulphur; that is to say, two parts of the water, or at the most three, with one of the pure Sulphur, ground and purged.

N.B.—But it is better that thou takest two parts to one.

16. *The Working of the Mixture at a Manual Operation.*

This thy mixture thou shalt grind very well upon a marble; then thou shalt wash it with vinegar and *Sal Ammoniac*, until it hath put off all its black fæces; then thou shalt wash off all its saltness and acrimony with clear fountain water; then shalt thou dry it upon clean white paper, by turning of it from place to place with the point of a knife, even unto an exquisite dryness.

17. *The Putting in of the Fetus into the Philosophical Egg.*

Now thy mixture being dried, put it into an oval glass, of the best and most transparent glass, of the bigness of a hen's egg; in such a glass let not thy matter exceed two ounces: seal it hermetically.

18. *The Government of the Fire.*

Then you must have a furnace built, in which you may keep an immortal fire; in it you shall make a heat of sand of the first degree, in which the dew of our compound may be elevated and circulated continually, day and night, without any intermission, etc. And in such a fire the body will die, and the spirit will be renewed; and at length the soul will be glorified and united with a new immortal and incorruptible body.

Thus is made a new Heaven.

FINIS.

www.ingramcontent.com/pod-product-compliance
Lightning Source LLC
Chambersburg PA
CBHW071226160426
43196CB00012B/2424